Jokes For Nurses:
50 Jokes & Shift Notes

Jane John-Nwankwo RN

Copyright © 2014 by Jane John-Nwankwo RN, MSN

All rights reserved. No part of this book may be reproduced or transmitted in any form or by any means without written permission from the author.

ISBN-13: 978-1505730388

ISBN-10: 1505730384

Printed in the United States of America.

OTHER TITLES FROM THE SAME AUTHOR:

1. ACLS Provider Manual
2. Work At Home Jobs for Nurses
3. How to make a million in Nursing
4. Crisis Prevention & Intervention in Healthcare
5. Choosing a Healthcare Career
6. EKG Technician Study Guide
7. Director of Staff Development: The Nurse Educator
8. Personality Types
9. Medical Assistant Test Preparation
10. How to Start Your Own Business
11. How to Grow Your Small Business
12. NRP Provider Manual

To order,
Visit
www.janejohn-nwankwo.com
www.djngbooks.org

let us laugh it off, nurses!

Joke 1. While working as a student nurse, Christy came across an elderly gentleman sitting on the edge of the bed in a room she was passing by. His suitcase was packed and sitting at his feet. Christy insisted on helping the sweet elderly man into a wheel chair so that he could be taken downstairs in a wheel chair, as is the hospital policy for patients who are being discharged.

Despite his protests, and after a quick chat about rules being rules, he reluctantly let Christy wheel him to the elevator. On the ride down to the lobby, Christy asked if his wife was meeting him.

"I don't know if she'll know where to find me!" He said! "She's still upstairs in the bathroom, changing out of her hospital gown!"

"The friend in my adversity I shall always cherish most. I can better trust those who helped to relieve the gloom of my dark hours than those who are so ready to enjoy with me the sunshine of my prosperity."

— **Ulysses S. Grant**

Joke 2. Shawn and Leslie were both patients in a mental health facility. They struck up a friendship that led to daily walks together. One day while they were walking past the facility swimming pool, Shawn suddenly leapt into the deep end. He sank straight down to the bottom of the pool and there he stayed. Leslie promptly jumped in, swam to the bottom of the pool, and heroically pulled Shawn out. When the head nurse head of Leslie's bravery, she immediately went about ordering her discharge from the mental health hospital, as she now considered Leslie to be mentally stable.

The head nurse went in to tell Leslie the great news, "Leslie, I have good news and bad news. The good news is you're being discharged; since you were able to rationally respond to a crisis by jumping in and saving the life of another patient. I have concluded that your act displays sound mindedness. The bad news is that Shawn hung himself with his bathrobe belt in his bathroom. I'm so sorry."

Leslie replied happily, "He didn't hang himself. I put him there to dry. How soon can I go home?"

SHIFT DUTY REMINDERS

"OUR HUMAN COMPASSION BINDS US THE ONE TO THE OTHER - NOT IN PITY OR PATRONIZINGLY, BUT AS HUMAN BEINGS WHO HAVE LEARNT HOW TO TURN OUR COMMON SUFFERING INTO HOPE FOR THE FUTURE."

— **NELSON MANDELA**

www.janejohn-nwankwo.com

www.djngbooks.org

Joke 3. On a busy surgical floor, the doctor stops the nurse to brief her on a patient's condition. "This patient is a fellow physician and my favorite golf partner. His injury is serious and I fear he will not be able to play golf again unless you follow my orders exactly." The doctor then began listing orders:

"You must give an injection in a different location every twenty minutes followed by a second injection exactly five minutes after the first. He must take two pills at exactly every hour followed by one pill every fifteen minutes for eight hours. He must drink no more and no less than ten ounces of water every twenty-five minutes and must void between. Soak his arm in warm water every fifteen minutes then place ice for ten minutes and repeat over and over for the rest of the day. Give range of motion every thirty minutes. He requires a back rub and foot rub every hour. Feed him something tasty every hour. Be cheerful and do whatever he asks at all times. Chart his condition and vital signs every twenty minutes. You must do these things exactly as I ordered or his injury will not heal properly, and he will not able to play golf well."

The nurse left the doctor and entered the patient's room. She was greeted by an anxious family and an equally anxious patient. The nurse started, "The doctor said that you will live." Then quickly reviewing the orders, the nurse added, "But you will have to learn a new sport."

"Good is somebody who delivered and allowed the company to overcome obstacles, without leaving a profound impact on its culture. Great is somebody who leads his company to achievements and performance and value that nobody was expecting it had."

— **Carlos Ghosn**

Joke 4. A nursing assistant, floor nurse and charge nurse from a small nursing facility were taking a lunch break in the break room. In walked a lady dressed in designer clothing, and wearing plenty of flashy jewelry.

"I am Sophia, a great and powerful witch!" she said. "I am so pleased with the way you have taken care of my aunt that I will now grant each of you a wish!"

With a wave of her hand and a puff of smoke, the room was filled with flowers and lavish gifts, as a show of her ability to grant wishes.

The nurses quickly decided who would ask for their wish first; the nursing assistant wished first. "I wish I were on a tropical island beach, with gorgeous men tending to my every need!" With a puff of smoke, the nursing assistant was gone.
The floor nurse went next. "I wish I were rich and retired; spending my days in my own warm cabin at a ski resort with a gorgeous man tending to my every need!" With a puff of smoke, she too was gone.

The charge nurse stood up and said," I want those two back on the floor at the end of the lunch break."

SHIFT DUTY NOTES

"Thousands of candles can be lit from a single candle, and the life of the candle will not be shortened. Happiness never decreases by being shared."

— **buddha**

www.janejohn-nwankwo
www.djngbooks.org

Joke 5. A well-known and very wealthy businessman had to spend a couple of days in the hospital. He was a royal pain to the nurses caring for him, and was incredibly rude to each of them. After the nurses refused to continue taking abuse from him, the head nurse took over his care.

She came into his room and announced, "I have to take your temperature." After complaining for several minutes about shoddy nursing care, he finally settled down, crossed his arms and opened his mouth.

"Sorry, sir. For this reading, I cannot use an oral thermometer." This started another round of complaining, but eventually he rolled over and bared his rear end. After feeling the nurse insert the thermometer, he heard her announce, "I have to get your meds. Now you stay JUST LIKE

THAT until I get back!"

She left the door to his room open as she walked out. He cursed under his breath as he heard people walking past his door laughing. After almost an hour, the man's doctor comes into the room. "What's going on here?" asked the doctor. Angrily, the man answers, "Haven't you ever seen someone having their temperature taken?" After a pause, the doctor confesses, "Well, no. I guess I haven't. Not with a carnation, at any rate."

SHIFT DUTY NOTES

Joke 6. Her first day on the job, a nurse brought a lunch tray to Ole Bubba Smith, who was in hospital

recovering after surgery. She also brought in a urine specimen cup, stating that when he could, he should fill up the cup.

Now Ole Bubba Smith had never really been a regular patient before he needed surgery, so when he saw the apple juice on his lunch tray, he put two and two together. He used his clean cup to pour his apple juice into.

When his nurse came in to collect the specimen cup she held it up and said to Ole Bubba, "The color is a bit off, are you feeling okay?" Ole Bubba reached for the cup and said, "Well, let me check!" After looking at it, he shrugged, "Looks good to me." He drank the contents of the cup in one big swig. The nurse fainted.

Joke 7. An elderly gentleman and his daughter went to see a Nurse Practitioner for the gentleman's monthly checkup. During the examination, the Nurse Practitioner asked about his nightly incontinence, as it had been an issue he'd mentioned on prior visits.

"Everything's fine now," said the man. "I just get up and go to the bathroom! God turns on the light for me; I do my business and go back to bed!"

After the examination, the Nurse Practitioner called the daughter in, to discuss her concerns about the gentleman's mental facilities, because he believes God is turning on the bathroom light for him.

The daughter went pale, "Oh no! He's been peeing in the fridge again! I did wonder why he kept spilling apple juice every night!"

www.janejohn-nwankwo.com
www.djngbooks.org

Joke 8. Just before he was scheduled to go in for surgery, a man was seen frantically wheeling himself down the hospital hallway toward the nearest exit. A nurse ran and stopped him. She asked him what the problem was. With a shaking voice, the man said, "I heard my nurse say, 'It's a just a very simple procedure! Don't worry; I'm sure it will be all right.'"

The nurse in front of him smiled and said, "She was just trying to comfort you, that's her job! There's nothing to worry about there!"

The man looked panicked, "She wasn't talking to me. She was talking to the surgeon!"

Joke 9. Very early one morning my husband, who runs a funeral home, woke me up with complaints of severe pain. I rushed him to the emergency room, where the staff ran a battery of tests to determine what could be causing his terrible pain.

My husband and I had discussed on the way to the hospital that I wouldn't call in sick for him until we could verify what the cause of the pain was; we hoped that it was something that could be treated easily.

The results came back, and the nurse told us that my husband had kidney stones, and would need immediate treatment to relieve his pain.

I turned to my husband and said to him, "I'm going to call the funeral home right now."

The nurse looked concerned, "Oh no, honey! He's not that sick!"

SHIFT DUTY NOTES

---

10. A woman went to see her doctor for her yearly physical. The doctor's nurse started with the basics, "Okay, how much do you weigh? She asked.

The woman smiled, "135lbs."

The nurse had her step on the scale, where her weight was a shocking 165lbs. The woman frowned, but said nothing.

The nurse asked, "How tall are you?"

"I'm 5'11"," She responded.

The nurse had her patient lean up against a wall chart, where her height was actually 5'8". The woman gasped, but still said nothing.

The nurse sat her down to take her blood pressure, and said, "Oh dear. Your blood pressure is on the high end."

The woman huffed, "Of course it would be high! When I came in here I was tall and slim! Now I'm just short and frumpy!"

"The friend who can be silent with us in a moment of despair or confusion, who can stay with us in an hour of grief and bereavement, who can tolerate not knowing... not healing, not curing... that is a friend who cares."

— **Henri Nouwen**

"Surround yourself with good people. People who are going to be honest with you and look out for your best interests."

— **Derek Jeter**

"Motivation is what gets you started. Habit is what keeps you going."

— **Jim Rohn**

11. A family took their elderly mother to a nursing home so that she could get the care they couldn't provide to her at home. The very next morning the elderly lady was bathed, dressed, fed a sumptuous breakfast, and set outside in a picturesque flower garden.

A nurse was nearby, watching her patients as they enjoyed their time outside, and she noticed the elderly lady started to lean sideways in her wheelchair. The attentive nurse rushed over and straightened her up. A few minutes later, the elderly lady started to lead sideways again. The nurses rushed over and put her right so that she didn't tip over! This went on several more times, until the woman's family arrived to check on her.

"How are they treating you,

grandma?" asked the elderly woman's granddaughter, as she took in the nice facility. The elderly woman sighed, "It's lovely, really. They just won't let me fart!"

12. A nurse carefully took her patient back to his room after a routine surgery, so that he could recover in the comfort and silence of his private room. The patient was still feeling the effects of the anesthesia, and was a little bit confused about where he was. After the nurse had made her patient as comfortable as possible, she allowed the man's family to come in and keep him company as he recovered from his procedure.

"How is he doing, nurse?" The man's wife asked.

The nurse replied helpfully, "He is quite dopey."

The wife nodded seriously, "Yes, we all know that. But how is he doing physically?"

13. Susan worked as a pediatric nurse in a busy pediatrician's office. One of her less than pleasant tasks was to be the one who administered shots to her 'littlest' patients. One day she entered the examination room to give a set of routine vaccinations to a little girl.

The little girl started screaming at the top of her lungs once she saw Susan entering the room, "No! No! No!"

The little girl's mother said, shocked, "Jane! That's not a polite behavior! We use our manners!"

The little girl paused, looked thoughtful and then continued her screaming, "No thank you! No thank you! No thank you!"

14. Two doctors were reviewing charts, and complaining about the new nurse, Nurse Lizzy.
"She's incredibly mixed up," said one

doctor. "She does everything absolutely backwards.
Just last week, I told her to give a patient 2 milligrams of morphine every 10 hours.
She gave him 10 milligrams every 2 hours. We damn near lost him!"
The second doctor said, "That's nothing. Earlier this week, I told her to give a patient an enema every 24 hours. She tried to give him 24 enemas in one hour! The guy damn near exploded!"
Suddenly, they heard a blood-curdling scream from down the hall. "Oh my God!" said the first doctor, "I just realized I told Nurse Lizzy to prick Mr. Smith's boil!"

15. A woman went to visit her 95 year old grandfather in his new nursing home. "How are you doing, grandpa?" she asked. The elderly man smiled, "I'm feeling great! The food is terrific, the nurses really take care of me!"

The woman felt relieved that her grandfather was being well cared for, "How are you sleeping? Are you still having a problem with insomnia?"

Her grandfather shook his head, "Not anymore! I get a solid nine hours of sleep, each night. At 10PM the nurse brings me a lovely cup of hot cocoa, and a Viagra tablet. I go out like a light after that!"

The woman is confused, and a little bit concerned. She rushed off to question the nurses charged with caring for her grandfather, "Please tell me you aren't really giving a 95 year old man

Viagra every day?"

"Oh yes!" nodded the nurse. "Every night we give our male patients a cup of hot cocoa and the Viagra. The nice soothing hot cocoa helps them drift off to sleep, and the Viagra helps to keep them from rolling out of bed."

SHIFT DUTY NOTES

"Success is walking from failure to failure with no loss of enthusiasm."

— **Winston Churchill**

16. Hank found himself having medical problems of a delicate nature, and went into town to meet with his doctor. His doctor had a new nurse, a young lady right out of nursing school. The nurse started going through Hank's medical history and list of medications, and then asked him why he was there to see the doctor today.

Hank stammered a little bit, "It's kind of personal. I would rather just tell the doctor." The nurse sighed, "Telling me what the problem is will help to speed things up when the doctor gets in here." Hank said, "Ok. Well I'm having some trouble with my penis…" The nurse's face turned beet red, and she rushed out of the room.

The doctor came in and explained, "She's a delicate old-fashioned kind of lady. The next time, just tell her that you have a problem with your foot, and when I come in, I'll know what you're here to see me about."

Three days later, Hank returned to his doctor because his problems had still not cleared up. The same nurse asked Hank why he was there to see the doctor, and Hank responded, "I'm having a problem with my right foot."

The nurse frowned and asked, "What kind of problems are you having?"

Hank grinned, "I can't pee out of it!"

"The smallest act of kindness is worth more than the grandest intention."

— **Oscar Wilde**

17. A nurse was tending to her patients in a busy office, when a nun came racing out of the exam room, yelling and crying. She was so visibly upset that she just ran out and slammed the door behind her.

The doctor came out of the exam room, shaking his head. The nurse asked him, "Doctor, what the heck happened in there?"

The doctor smiled, "I examined her, and then I told her that she was pregnant."

The nurse gasped, "But she's a nun! Surely that can't be right, doctor! There must be some mistake"

The doctor laughed, "She's not pregnant. But it certainly did cure her hiccups!"

How to Make
A MILLION
in Nursing

The First 5 steps

Jane John-Nwankwo RN, MSN

www.janejohn-nwankwo.com

www.djngbooks.org

18. Four men were pacing in the labor and delivery waiting room, in a Minneapolis hospital, while their wives gave birth.

A nurse entered the room and announced to one of the men, "Congrats! You've got twins!" "Wow, what a coincidence," the man said. "I

work for the Minnesota Twins baseball franchise!"

The nurse came back a little while later and said to the second man, "Congrats! You've got triplets!" "Wow, that's wild," said the new dad. "I work for the 3M Corporation!"

An hour later the nurse returned and said to the third man, "Congrats! You've got quadruplets!" The new dad was stunned, "What an amazing coincidence, I work for the Four Seasons Hotel!"

Suddenly there was a thud behind him, and they all turned to see that the fourth expectant father had fainted. The nurse rushed over and sat with him until he'd come around again, "Are you all right, sir?!" The man took a deep breath, "I'm okay. With all of these coincidences, it occurred to me, I work for 7-11."

19. It was her very first day working at the nursing home. Nurse Ann was doing her rounds and checking on her first patient of the day. Her first patient was an elderly woman who smiled and said, "Good morning, nurse. Just to let you know that I'm slightly deaf, so speak up!" Nurse Ann smiled and nodded, "I'm just going to take your vitals."

The elderly patient waited while Nurse Ann took her temperature, took her blood pressure, and then placed a stethoscope on her chest. "Big breaths," instructed Nurse Ann. The elderly woman nodded sadly, "Yes. Yes, they used to be!"

20. Three doctors and three nurses were traveling by train, to attend a medical conference. At the train station, each of the doctors purchased a ticket. They watched in surprise as the nurses purchased only one ticket between them. "How are you all going to travel on one ticket?" the doctors asked.

"Just watch, and you'll see!" Answered one of the nurses. All of them boarded the train, and the doctors went to their seats. They watched in interest as all three nurses crammed themselves into the restroom and closed the door behind them. Shortly after the train left the station, the conductor came around to collect tickets. He knocked on the restroom door and said, "Ticket, please." The door opened just a crack, and an arm emerged holding out a ticket. The conductor took the ticket and moved on.

The doctors agreed that this was quite a clever idea. After the conference, the doctors decided to use the same plan to save some money off their own tickets. They got to the train station and bought one ticket. To their surprise, the nurses didn't buy even a single ticket for their return trip.

The doctors were perplexed, "How are you going to get home now?" They asked. The nurses just smiled and said, "You'll see."

When they boarded the train the three doctors jammed themselves into one restroom, and the three nurses jammed themselves into another. When the train departed the station one of the nurses made her way to the restroom where the doctors were hiding. She knocked on the door and said, "Ticket, please!"

SHIFT REMINDERS

"Whoever is careless with the truth in small matters cannot be trusted with important matters."

— **Albert Einstein**

www.janejohn-nwankwo.com

www.djngbooks.org

21. A doctor wanted to be very nice to his nurses. He took time to bake 'rock balls'. He happily brought the oven fresh balls to the nurses' lounge and shouted loudly "Hey Everyone, come eat my balls!" All the nurses were speechless. Finally Nurse Nancy said "Your-r BALLS?" "Yes", he replied. They are "Rock balls".

22. A hospital's intensive care unit started experiencing a rash of unexplained patient deaths. Each death occurred on Monday morning at 9am, regardless of the medical conditions the patients were recovering from. This was absolutely baffling the doctors and nurses who were treating the patients; some had even started to think that something supernatural was going on.

The hospital brought in an international expert to help them get to the bottom of the mystery. A few minutes before 9am on Monday morning, the medical staff waited nervously around the ICU; all waiting to see what would happen. The clock ticked to 9am and they heard alarms going off. The medical team ran to the side of their patient, but it was too late.

The following Monday the same thing happened. The doctors and nurses shook their heads, and started to think that maybe it really was a supernatural issue. They were just leaving the ICU and saw the hospital's new cleaning woman bending down, unplugging the vacuum cleaner, and plugging the life-support machines back in...

www.janejohn-nwankwo.com

www.djngbooks.org

"Man often becomes what he believes himself to be. If I keep on saying to myself that I cannot do a certain thing, it is possible that I may end by really becoming incapable of doing it. On the contrary, if I have the belief that I can do it, I shall surely acquire the capacity to do it even if I may not have it at the beginning."

— **Mahatma Gandhi**

23. A nurse was excited to start her new job at a hospital. She was learning the ropes, and was startled to hear a doctor yell out, "Tetanus! Measles! Mumps! Smallpox!"

The nurse was confused, but ignored it. An hour later she was startled once again when the doctor suddenly yelled out, "Rubella! Pertussis! Influenza!"

The nurse was very confused now, and curiosity was getting the better of her. She turned to the other nurse working with her and asked, "What's he doing?"

The other nurse sighed and shook her head, "Oh, he just likes to call the shots around here."

24. Michelle was a beautiful nurse, with an amazing body and a winning smile. She was having trouble at work, so went to see one of the resident psychiatrists in the hospital she worked in. "Doctor, you have to please help me!" she begged. The psychiatrist looked concerned, "What's going on, Michelle?" she asked.

Michelle sighed, "I have such a problem. Every time I meet one of the gorgeous young doctors here, I wind up dating him and then dumping him; breaking his heart. Then I spend weeks feeling guilty about it.

The psychiatrist nodded, "I see. So you

need help so that you can have the willpower needed to stop dating those handsome young men?"

Nurse Michelle shook her head, "No! I just want you to help me avoid feeling guilty and depressed afterwards!"

SHIFT REMINDERS

----

25. Three nurses died, and found themselves at the Pearly Gates, being met by St. Peter. To the first nurse, St.

Peter said, "What did you do during your time on earth, and why should you enter into heaven?"

The first nurse looked modest, "I was a nurse in an inner city hospital. I worked tirelessly to bring health and healing to the inner city children." St. Peter nodded, "Very admirable. You may enter." The nurse passed through the Pearly Gates.

To the second nurse, he asked the same question. The nurse responded, "I was a volunteer nurse in the poorest parts of Africa. With a skeleton crew, we brought a hand of healing to those who needed it most. St. Peter looked impressed, "That is amazing. You may enter.

To the third nurse, St. Peter once again asked the question. The third nurse replied, after a moment of hesitation, "I was a nurse at an H.M.O." St. Peter frowned and paused for a minute, then said, "Ok, you may enter."

"Oh thank goodness," said the nurse. "For a moment there I thought that you weren't going to let me in!" St. Peter gestured through the Pearly Gates, "You can come in, yes. But you can only stay for three days."

26. A nurse died and went to heaven. She finds herself at the Pearly Gate, met by St. John. St. John asked her questions about her life. She was answering the questions honestly, but then spotted a man sitting on a cloud behind the gates. He was wearing a white coat, with a stethoscope around his neck.

"Is that a doctor?" She asked. "I was

just working at a hospital with some really high-maintenance doctors who made the lives of us nurses rather challenging!"

27. Four nurses have had it with the doctor that they work with. His arrogant and rude behavior to them was no longer bearable. They decide to all play some practical jokes on him. Later in the day, they all meet at a restaurant to discuss what they'd done to the arrogant doctor.

The first nurse said, "I stuffed cotton into his stethoscope so he couldn't hear!"

The second nurse said, "I took the mercury out of his thermometers, and painted them all to read 120 degrees!"

The third nurse said, "Wow, I did something a little bit more daring. I poked holes in all of the condoms that I found in his desk drawer."

The fourth nurse fainted.

SHIFT REMINDERS

---

28. A Nurse Practitioner and a lawyer were chatting at a charity event. Their conversations were constantly interrupted by people coming up to the nurse, describing their ailments, and asking for free medical advice.

After about an hour, the frustrated Nurse Practitioner turned to the lawyer and said, "What do you do to stop people from asking you for free legal advice?"

The lawyer smiled, "I give them the advice, happily. And then I send them a bill."

The nurse was surprised, but by the end of the evening she was ready to give it a try. At the end of the week, still feeling a little bit guilty, she prepared bills to send to those who'd asked her for advice while she was trying to enjoy an evening. She walked out to the mailbox to put the bills into it. And found a bill from the lawyer.

29. A nurse was having a very busy shift, so much so that she just didn't have time to eat dinner. She walked into a patient's bedroom and found him asleep. Taking a bit of a break, she sat down and noticed that he had a bowl of raisins on a table next to him. Starved, she grabbed a few handfuls before getting ready to check her patient's vitals.

The patient woke up when she started to take his blood pressure. She smiled at her patient, "I'm sorry, I had a few of your raisins. I was so hungry."

The patient smiled back, "That's okay, nurse. After I've sucked all of the chocolate off, I don't like them much anyway."

www.janejohn-nwankwo.com

www.djngbooks.org

30. Mr. Byrd was in hospital recovering from surgery. His doctor came in, muttered a few words at his patient and left before Mr. Byrd could get any of his questions answered. The same thing happened that afternoon, which left Mr. Byrd very frustrated.

The nursing station received a phone call that evening, from a gentleman asking after Mr. Byrd's health. The nurse told the caller, "His surgery went great; he is recovering wonderfully, and should be discharged in another day. Do you want to talk to Mr. Byrd himself now?"

The caller laughed, "Ha! This is Mr. Byrd! The doctors don't tell me anything!"

31. Nurse Lindsey worked at a nursing home. She was told that she had a new elderly patient to care for, so she went to see her new patient. After introducing herself to the patient, Nurse Lindsey went down a list of routine questions, including questions about the patient's medical history and her current concerns.

She noticed that her patient had limited mobility, due to an injury. "Mrs. Davis, how long has it been since you were bedridden?"

To Nurse Lindsey's surprise, her patient blushed beet red and stammered, "That's a rather personal question," she said.

Being a sensitive nurse, she responded, "You can tell me anything, Mrs. Davis."

Her patient shrugged, "Well, I would say it has been about 20 years. Since my husband was alive."

32. Nurse Steve was assigned to care for a new patient who was visiting the lovely state of Kentucky, from Australia. He walked into the patient's room and saw she was just finishing up her breakfast, "So how was your breakfast this morning?" he asked.

The patient shrugged, "It was very good, but I just can't seem to get used to the jelly that you put on your toast."

Nurse Steve looked confused, "What flavor was the jelly?" he asked.

The patient handed over a foil packet, "It's this Kentucky Jelly." The label on the foil packet read "KY Jelly."

33. A new young doctor was doing his residency on the OB floor of a hospital. The nurse accompanying him on rounds had a ton of experience and knew a nervous doctor when she saw one. She quickly gathered that he was feeling a little bit of embarrassment when performing routing pelvic exams on his female patients. She offered him a little tip to help him relax, "Just whistle a tune, and it'll help you to focus better, while helping your embracement.

The doctor agreed that this was a good tactic. He started going about examining his next patient, and softly hummed the first tune that popped into his head. He stopped, startled, when both the nurse and his patient burst out laughing.

Thoroughly humiliated, he asked, "What is going on?!" The nurse tried to smother her laughter as she responded, "The tune you're whistling is "I wish I was an Oscar Meyer Wiener."

34. A fireman was lying on his hospital bed after an accident while he was at work fighting a fire. He had an oxygen mask covering his mouth when a nursing student came in to check on him and sponge away some of the soot and dirt from his hands and face.

"Nurse," he mumbled from behind the mask, "Are my testicles black?"

The young nursing student blushed furiously, "I don't know. I'm just here to get you a little cleaned up."

The fireman repeated, forcing his words out, "Please, are my testicles black?"

The on duty nurse walked into the room and saw the patient looking frustrated and anxious, "What's going on?" she asked.

The patient repeated, "Please, nurse. Are my testicles black?"

The nurse was undaunted and whipped back the sheet and took a good look, "Everything looks great, sir. There's nothing to worry about."

The man struggles to sit up finally, and

pulls off his oxygen mask with some difficulty, "I asked if my test results were back!"

www.janejohn-nwankwo.com

www.djngbooks.org

35. Feeling embarrassed about a problem he was having, Charlie went to a clinic. He sat down with the nurse, "Nurses are professionals, right? Even if the problem is embarrassing, you won't laugh?"

The nurse was offended, "Of course I won't laugh! I've been a nurse for over twenty years. I have seen it all."

Joe felt relieved. He stood up and dropped his trousers, only to reveal the smallest male appendage that the nurse had ever seen. The nurse struggled to maintain her sense of professionalism, but found that giggles were escaping. She left the room quickly, but came back once she'd gained her composure, "I'm so sorry. That won't happen again. Please, tell me what the problem is."

Charlie sighed, "It's swollen."

SHIFT REMINDERS

----

36. A gorgeous young woman brought her much older husband into the hospital, telling the nurse that he was having chest pains, sweating profusely, and having difficulty catching his breath. The nurse took them to a room and went about making the older gentleman as comfortable as possible. She looked at the patient's wife, "I have to tell you Mrs. Cole, I really don't like the way that your husband looks.

The younger wife shrugged and filed her nails, "I don't like the way that he looks either. But he's rich, and he put me in the will as his sole heir."

37. A man who was married to a nurse was having a few beers with his buddies. They were all kidding around, and one of his buddies said, "I bet it's great being married to a nurse." The man sighed, "It's harder to live with a nurse than you'd imagine. When you forget to flush the toilet, you get a complete analysis, with a diet plan to correct any problems. Thanksgiving dinners is cut up into small pieces, because she doesn't want to have to do the Heimlich in case someone chokes, and ruins her only day off in months. And I've been awakened from a deep slumber to find her shaking me because my breathing patterns were just a little too close to a Cheyne-Stokes rhythm!

38. A motorcycle cop with a reputation for pulling people over for almost any or no reason is rushed into hospital with an inflamed appendix. The surgery goes smoothly and his surgeon reassures him that the procedure went well, and he should recover swiftly.

While in recovery, the cop feels something pulling painfully at his chest hairs. Worried that there is a new problem, he slowly moves his hospital gown so that he can take a look at his chest. He is startled to see three wide strips of adhesive tape across his very hairy chest, with a note written on the tape, "Get well quick, from the nurses you pulled over last week!"

He pulled the first strip of tape off and screamed at the agony. Just then, he noticed that his groin area was feeling just as uncomfortable as his chest first was. He pulled back his gown and noticed three more strips of tape. His screams could be heard three counties over.

39. A Brooklyn hospital found itself at odds with the doctors on staff, over a number of concerns. One day all of the doctors decided to go on strike, leaving the hospital with a severe problem. Media outlets ran to cover the story, the hospital's representative agreed to do an interview. He sat down with the reporter, who asked, "Have the doctors stated what their demands are yet? How do you plan on addressing this problem with them?

The hospital representative sat up and cleared his throat, "We are not really sure, right now, what they are asking for."

Confused, the reporter asked, "Well surely someone is communicating with the striking doctors?"

The hospital rep sighed, "Well, we're really waiting for a nurse to be free so that someone will be able to read the picket signs!"

Janet Smith

Affiliate Marketing

www.janejohn-nwankwo.com

40. A man went to see his doctor, but when he arrived at the office he was told by the doctor's rather attractive nurse, "The doctor is at the hospital on an emergency. He won't be back for about an hour."

The man sighed, "Ok, well I just was feeling very tense, and wanted to see if he could prescribe something to help me."

The nurse looked at the man, with an appraising eye, decided he was very attractive. "I've got just the thing for you! For $100, I'll cure your tension!" The man agreed, and the nurse proceeded to... It was the best experience he'd ever had.

A week later, he returned to the doctor's office, only to find that the doctor was in. The doctor listened to his symptoms, and wrote out a prescription for medication to help his stress and tension. The doctor said, "That'll be $200 for the visit."

The man smiles and says, "If it's all the same to you, doctor, I'd much rather have the $100 cure!"

41. A man was feeling terribly sick and finally went to see his doctor. The doctor said, "Nothing much to worry about, you've just got a touch of a pneumonia. I'll prescribe some medications, you get plenty of rest, and you'll be up and on your feet in no time at all!"

The man was very worried, "Are you sure it's just pneumonia? I once heard of a guy who had pneumonia but died of a heart attack."

The doctor's nurse patted the man on his hand, "It'll be okay, really. When Doctor Harris treats someone who has pneumonia, the patient will die of pneumonia."

SHIFT REMINDERS

www.janejohn-nwankwo.com

www.djngbooks.org

"You have not lived today until you have done something for someone who can never repay you."

— **John Bunyan**

42. A woman went to see her doctor because she was suffering from a terrible sinus infection. Her doctor prescribed some medications, but a week later she was back still as sick as can be. This time the doctor gave her a shot, but that didn't seem to do any good either.

On the third visit, the doctor told his patient, "You need to go home, take a hot bath, and then throw all of the windows open and stand in the cold winter air!"

The woman was shocked, "But, if I do that I'm sure to get pneumonia!"

The doctor's nurse sighed and said to the bewildered patient, "Yes, but he can cure pneumonia."

43. After working a double shift that was truly a nightmare of a night, an exhausted nurse walked into the bank to sign some paperwork on a loan for her new house. Getting ready to sign the paperwork, she reached into her purse and pulled out a rectal thermometer. She tried to sign the paperwork, but quickly saw that she was holding the thermometer! The loan manager raised an eyebrow and said, "You might do better with a pen?"

The embarrassed nurse realized her mistake and looked at the confused loan manager, "Well that's just perfect. Just perfect! Some ass has got my pen!"

44. A young man went to the local clinic for some chronic pain. He met with the Nurse Practitioner who started with her standard questions. "Where are you hurting the most?" she asked.

The man cried out, "Oh you just have to help me. I hurt all over. Every part of my body hurts!"

The Nurse Practitioner looked a little bit worried, "What do you mean all over? Can you show me?"

The mam touched his right knee with his index finger and yelled out, "Ouch! See!" Then he touched his cheek and cried out, "Oh it hurts! It hurts everywhere!"

The Nurse Practitioner looked thoughtful and said to her worried patient, "Stop poking yourself. You have a broken finger."

45. A doctor was having a torrid affair with his nurse. Soon she told him that she was pregnant. Not wanting his wife to know, he gave the nurse a sum of money and asked her to go to Italy and have the baby there. "But how will I let you know the baby is born?" she asked.

He replied, "Just send me a postcard and write "spaghetti" on the back. I'll take care of expenses." Not knowing what else to do, the nurse took the money and flew to Italy. Six months went by, and then one day the doctor's wife called him at the office and said, "Dear, you received a very strange postcard in the mail today from Europe, and I don't understand what it means."

The doctor sighed and said, "I will explain it to you when I get home." Later that evening the doctor came home, read the postcard, and fell to the floor with a heart attack. Paramedics rushed him to the hospital emergency room. The head medic stayed back to comfort the wife. He asked what trauma had precipitated the cardiac arrest. So the wife picked up the card and read: "Spaghetti, Spaghetti, Spaghetti, Spaghetti - Two with sausage and meatballs; two without."

46. The Top 6 Reasons to Become a Nurse

1. The pay is somewhat better than fast food, but the hours aren't as good.
2. The fashionable shoes and trendy scrubs ensure you always look your best.
3. Exposing yourself to countless viruses and infections, not to mention the various fluids that you are sure to find yourself encountering each day.
4. Learning to hone your people skills, while working side-by-side with grouchy doctors with illegible handwriting.
5. Hours of endless charting, which is sure to help you improve your own handwriting.

6. Being able to celebrate the holidays, at work, with your work friends.

47. A nursing student was doing rounds with her supervisor, and was baffled as to why the senior nurse would periodically use the rectal thermometer to get a temperature, but use the oral thermometer on some of the patients.

Finally, after about the 5th patient had been treated to the rectal thermometer, the nursing student asked, "Can you please explain to me how you know which patients you should use the rectal thermometer, and which ones are better served with the oral thermometer?

The older nurse smiled sweetly at her student, "It's just a little something I learned in nursing school."

After a few more patients, the student just had to know, "Please tell me so I can be sure to do the right thing!"

The older nurse said to her, "In nursing school they taught me to always look for my patient's best side when treating them!"

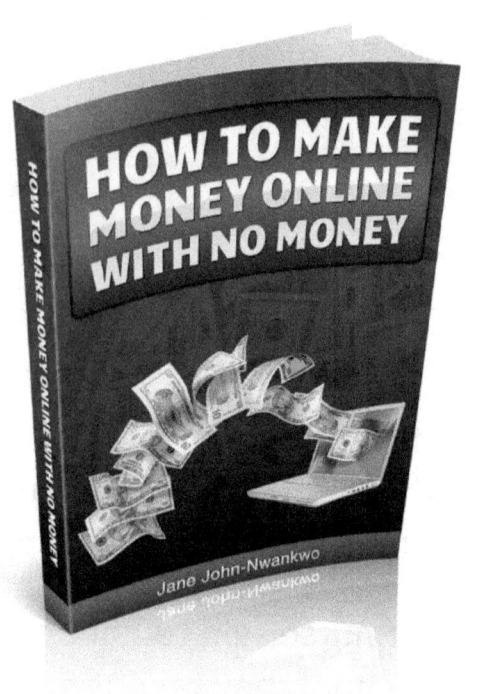

48. You might be a nurse if…

- When you use a public restroom, you find yourself washing your hands with soap for a full minute, and then turn the faucets off with your elbows.
- Everyone you meet tells you about all of their aches and pains, and

asks for treatment recommendations.
- You want to throw the TV out the window each time you see a nurse on TV gossiping or flirting with doctors.
- You can almost see the germs on doorknobs and telephones, not to mention public restrooms.
- You can watch the goriest movie and enjoy eating anything; including spaghetti!
- You have fantasies about telling doctors to clean up the most disgusting bedside messes.

49. How many nurse practitioners does it take to change a burned out light bulb? None, they just have a nursing assistant do it, and as many times as the doctor tells them that they need to have it changed.

How many triage nurses does it take

to change a burned out light bulb? One, but the burned out light bulb will have to spend four hours in the waiting room before the problem is diagnosed.

How many doctors does it take to change a burned out light bulb? Only one, but he has to have a nurse to tell him which end to screw in.

50. A cardiology patient worriedly said to his nurse, who was checking his IV, "I'm really concerned. Last week I read in the paper about a man who was in the hospital being treated for heart trouble, but then he died of meningitis!"

The nurse smiled and patted her patient's hand, "Relax! This is a fantastic first-rate hospital!"

The patient fidgeted and frowned,

"Are you sure? What about the cardiologist? Is he good?"

The nurse smiled again, "Of course he is! The heart trouble patients here either live or die!

SHIFT REMINDER NOTES

Jane John-Nwankwo RN, MSN

ACLS PROVIDER MANUAL
Study Guide For Advanced Cardiovascular Life Support

OTHER TITLES FROM THE SAME AUTHOR:

1. How to Make Money Online with No Money

2. Work At Home Jobs for Nurses

3. Crisis Prevention & Intervention in Healthcare

4. Choosing a Healthcare Career

5. Personality Types

6. Director of Staff Development: The Nurse Educator

7. How to Start Your Own Business

8. How to Grow Your Small Business

9. How to Mail Money Writing

10. EKG Interpretation

11. Phlebotomy Technician Technician Study Guide

12. How to make a million in nursing

To order,
Visit
www.janejohn-nwankwo.com
www.djngbooks.org

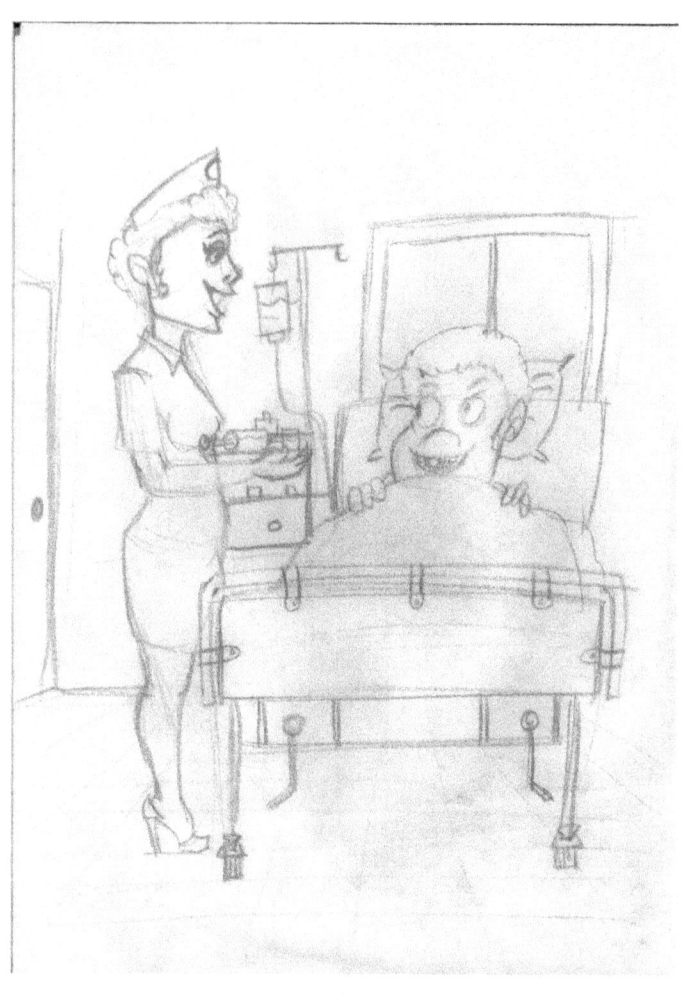

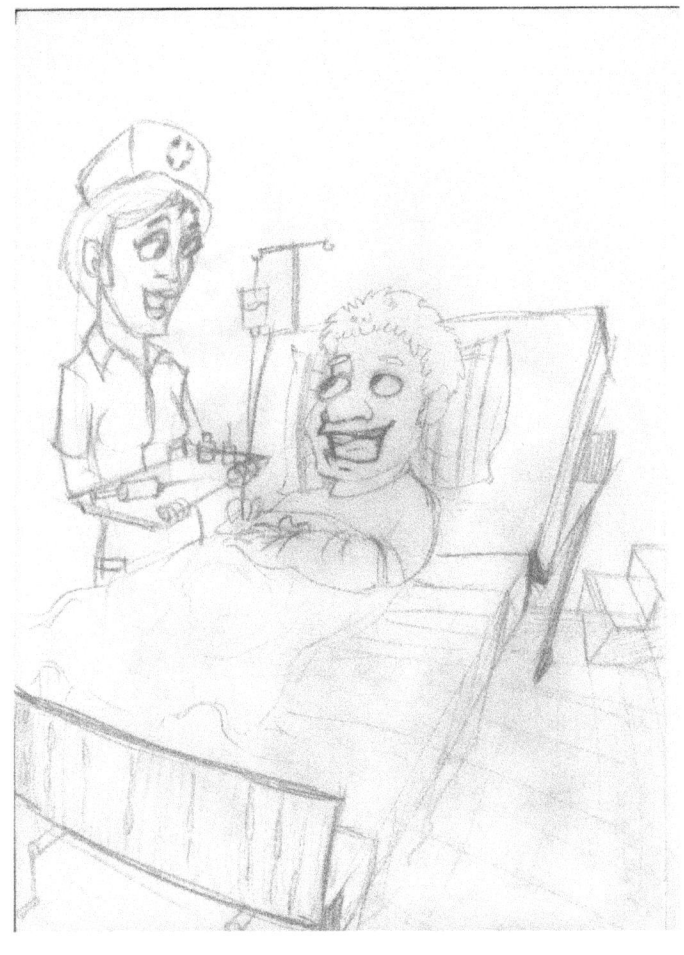

www.ingramcontent.com/pod-product-compliance
Lightning Source LLC
Chambersburg PA
CBHW051722170526
45167CB00002B/757